a *v*

Berr

Without the help of fellow ramblers none of the book could have been written down. Sincere thanks to-
Margaret Anderson, Erica Bamford, Arthur Bastow, Maggie Bates, Mike Fraser, Jill Hanham, Derrick Joannes, Stuart Lindley, Elliott Ray, Mike Symington, Annie Watt, Randi Wright, Phil Thompson, Julie Yellowley.
The book is more theirs than mine.
Particular thanks to Margaret, who tolerated my obsessive behaviour and encouraged me.
These friends lit up the dark times.

a walk round Berwick Borough

five castles, a palace and a mountain

Written and illustrated by
Arthur Wood

published by Berwick Ramblers

Published by Berwick Ramblers.
5 Quay Walls, Berwick-upon-Tweed.
TD15 1HB.
2006.

Written and illustrated by Arthur Wood.

Sketch maps are based on O.S Explorer Maps
and are reproduced by permission of Ordnance
Survey on behalf of HMSO.
© Crown Copyright 2006. All rights reserved.
Ordnance Survey Licence number 100033886.

ISBN : 0·9545331·1·9
(978·0·9545331·1·3)

Printed in Great Britain by Martins the Printers,
Sea View Works, Spittal, Berwick-upon-Tweed, TD15 1RS.
WWW. martins-the-printers·com

Berwick Borough
the lie of the land

approx. scale
6·25 ml.– 10 Km.

O.S. maps required for the route – 1:25 000 scale.
Explorer 346 – Berwick. Explorer 339 – Lower Tweed Valley.
Explorer OL 16 – the Cheviot Hills.
Explorer 332 – Alnwick & Amble. Explorer 340 – Holy Island.

Contents

Introduction

Berwick Borough, perched on the northern tip of England, is blessed with beautiful scenery and bears witness to a turbulent history. The present Borough was formed in 1974 by combining Berwick Municipal Borough with Norham and Islandshires Rural District, Belford Rural District and Glendale Rural District. Now we hear whisperings of Alnwick and Berwick being amalgamated, so this walking route will commemorate about 35 years of political endeavour. Reorganisation may present an opportunity to extend the walk.

At 120 miles, 192 km, the walk starts at Berwick-upon-Tweed and a bracing sea cliff stroll brings you to the Scottish Border, which is followed down to the River Tweed. Here the border runs up the mid-stream before it leaves the river to make for the Cheviot Hills. The Pennine Way conveniently follows the border fence over Whitelaw, the Black Hagg and the Schill, before climbing up the shoulder of "the muckle Cheviot," the highest mountain in Northumberland.

At the Hanging Stone the Borough boundary quits the national border and works its way through the rounded green Cheviot Hills to the Ingram Valley. An ancient track, Salters Road, provides good walking through the hills.

Beyond Ingram and Powburn the line crosses the Sandstone Ridge, with its rolling heather moors, heading for the North Sea.

CURLEW—
emblem of the
Northumberland
National Park

Long sandy beaches,
"Northumbria's Lordly
Strand," give an easy
route up the coast back
to the starting point
at Berwick.

The landscape varies
from sweeping golden
beaches and rugged sea
cliffs to leafy river
valleys and rolling
heather moors,
culminating in the
arctic wastes of
the Cheviot with its
blanket bog and inky quagmires,

Wildlife is plentiful and varied. The sparse
population of the Borough leaves space for
mother nature to survive and thrive.

The route follows rights of way, minor roads
and tracks, sometimes within the Borough,
sometimes outside it and occasionally on
the boundary itself.

It is divided into twelve day walks for those
who wish to tackle the route in a leisurely
manner. More ambitious walkers with
less time on their hands may reorganise
the walks into longer units, for instance
by saving 5 miles (8km.) if they combine
walks 5 and 6.

This is a walk past five medieval castles,
a palace and a mountain.

The sketch maps for each walk give limited information. It is recommended that walkers should also take the relevant Ordnance Survey Explorer map (orange cover). It gives much more information to help navigate the route. In bad weather the map can show escape routes. It can be used on a summit to identify prominent landmarks.

Walkers who are not familiar with navigating by map should gain some experience before tackling the Cheviots and the moors of the Sandstone Ridge. It is easy to follow the coast or riverbank, but the Cheviots are smooth green hills with little to differentiate one from another and accurate navigation is crucial.

You are unlikely to meet many farmers or local residents on these walks, but it is good policy to greet those you meet in a friendly manner. They are keen to know about you and can often give valuable information about conditions along the route.

Public transport to the start and finish of walks presents some difficulties, aggravated by recent cuts in service, so it is wise to cultivate the assistance of a non-walking motorist. Overnight accommodation can be scarce away from the popular coastal strip.

Berwick-upon-Tweed is the natural start and finish point of the circuit. It has a station on the main East Coast railway line served by G.N.E.R. and Virgin. There is a London to Edinburgh bus service and the A1 road runs through the Borough.

Berwick Borough has a good climate for walking. Spring and early Summer generally have reasonable temperatures, least rain and gentle winds. The prevailing westerly air flow brings moist air to the Cheviots, so precipitation there is much greater than on the easterly shore. The infamous bogs and marshy conditions on the broad summit of Cheviot bear witness to the heavier rainfall.

The Cheviot is 2,676 feet (815m) high and the temperature is lower at that altitude. Wind speed is also greater on the tops of the hills. It is important to be equipped with all the bad weather gear when venturing up Cheviot.

Visibility is generally good, but the Cheviots can be in cloud, giving thick wet mist and in early Summer the coast can be shrouded in North Sea haar.

The choice of footwear is all-important. Lightweight three-season boots with a degree of waterproofing and a good tread will suffice for all the walks. The coastal stretches could be walked in well-soled trainers.

Good quality wicking socks are essential to keep the feet dry. Many specialist socks are now on the market. Gaiters are good in wet weather on the moors.

A wind and waterproof coat and overtrousers are a necessity. Lightweight ones are useful as they are often stowed in your rucksack. A woolly hat and gloves for winter and a light weight hat for summer will take care of your head and hands.

Recent advances in clothing have introduced breathable base layers, insulating middle layers and weather proof outer layers. The choice of clothing can be bewildering, so take your time and choose wisely.

Not all walkers carry a survival bag, but as it can save your life on a remote walk, you should have one stowed in your bag. Also carry a whistle and a torch as well as a compass.

The sack should also contain emergency food such as dried fruit, chocolate bars or fruit cake. In winter a flask of your favourite hot drink and in summer plenty of water will keep you from dehydrating.

Those who walk on their own must leave details of their route and estimated return time with someone. This is not so important for a group, but it is good practice even then.

Mobile phones make it easier to summon help if you have an accident, but the middle of the Cheviots is outwith the range of some mobiles. In that situation the fittest member of the group will have to go to the nearest public phone (shown on O.S. maps). Sometimes a mobile signal can be got on higher ground.

If a walker is immobilised they should use the International distress call- six long blasts on a whistle, or flashes on a torch, repeated at minute intervals. Three short blasts at minute intervals is the response.

They should get into a sheltered spot, put on spare clothing and climb into the survival bag to maintain their body heat.

The best safety precaution is to walk carefully and watch where you're putting your feet.

Countryside Access

In England, in October 2005, the Countryside and Rights of Way Act (2000) introduced freedom to roam on foot over uncultivated land. O.S. explorer maps show access land tinted yellow. This walk follows rights of way, so the use of this access right is not essential, but it means that you can leave the right of way to investigate features of interest, or make a short cut, without fear of trespass.

THE COUNTRYSIDE CODE (England and Wales)

* Be safe - plan ahead and follow any signs.
* Leave gates and property as you find them.
* Protect plants and animals - take your litter home.
* Keep dogs under close control.
* Consider other people.

for more see www.countrysideaccess.gov.uk

In Scotland, in February 2005, the Land Reform (Scotland) Act (2003) established a statutory right of responsible access over most areas of land and water.

THE SCOTTISH OUTDOOR ACCESS CODE

When you're in the outdoors -

* Take personal responsibility for your own actions and act safely.
* Respect people's privacy and peace of mind.
* Help land managers and others to work safely and effectively.
* Care for your environment and take your litter home.
* Keep your dog under close control.
* Take extra care if you're organising an event or running a business.

for more see www.outdooraccess-scotland.com

Useful Addresses

England- Tourist Information Centres.
- BERWICK-upon-TWEED, 106 Marygate, TD15 1BN
  01289-330733. tourism@berwick-upon-tweed.gov.uk
- SEAHOUSES, Seafield Car Park, NE68 7SW.
  01665-720884. seahousesTIC@berwick-upon-tweed.gov.uk
- WOOLER, The Cheviot Centre, NE71 6BL.
  01668-282123. WoolerTIC@berwick-upon-tweed.gov.uk

SCOTLAND- Visitor Information Centres.
- EYEMOUTH, The Auld Kirk, Manse Rd., TD14 5JE
  (seasonal)
- KELSO, Town House, The Square, TD5 7HF.
or call 0870-6080404. www.visitscottishborders.com

Northumberland National Park.
- Ingram Visitor Centre.
or see northumberland-national-park.org.uk

Path and Access Information.
- Countryside Service.
  Northumberland County Council,
  County Hall, MORPETH, NE61 2EF.
  01670-533000. northumberland.gov.uk.

- Northumberland National Park.
  Eastburn, South Park, HEXHAM, NE46 1BS.
  01434-611675. northumberland-national-park.org.uk

- Scottish Borders Council Ranger Service,
  Harestanes, ANCRUM, TD8 6UQ.
  01835-830281.

the Walks

Walk One
Berwick to Mordington

A fine airy walk from Berwick to the Border, then a gentle climb up and over Lamberton Moor, shadowing the Border line on the Scottish side. This is a good walk for bird watchers and it should take 5 or 6 hours. Stout footwear is essential as there are narrow clifftop paths. Children and dogs must be closely controlled. The Berwickshire Coastal Path is followed for the first part of the walk. The walk is 8.5 miles (13.6 km.) long.

Start the walk at Bridge End – the Berwick end of the Old Bridge.

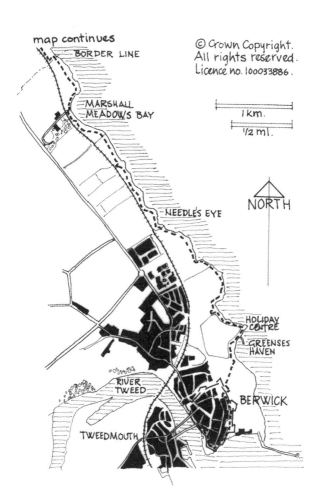

map continues

BORDER LINE

MARSHALL
MEADOWS BAY

1 km.

½ ml.

NORTH

NEEDLE'S EYE

HOLIDAY
CENTRE

GREENSES
HAVEN

RIVER
TWEED

BERWICK

TWEEDMOUTH

17

Facing the Town Hall spire, go right, cross the road and take the level footpath along the Quay Walls. The stone flagged walkway has Georgian houses on the left and a stout parapet on the right. Openings at Sallyport and Sandgate give unexpected views into the old town with its famous red roofs.

The path widens and curves past Wellington Terrace. On the right is Coxon's Tower and at Fishers Fort stands a Russian cannon, captured at the Crimea. The path passes over Nessgate, through a metal gate and up Kipper Hill. This is the start of the Elizabethan Ramparts, built to an Italian design as a defence against cannon.

Follow the level path past Windmill Bastion, shortly you will reach a big building on the left, it is Berwick Barracks, the first purpose-built barracks in the country.

COWPORT

.THE NEEDLE'S EYE

At the end of the barracks take a path down to the left, then go right to pass under the ramparts through Cowport, the only surviving original gateway in the ramparts.

Follow the road round to the left, past the bowling club, and take the road half right past the clubhouse, heading for the toilet block on the skyline. Go left at the toilets and follow the clifftop path in front of the massed caravans of the holiday centre. Down below a breakwater protects Greenses Haven. Keep past all the caravans, turning left along their northern boundary to a fingerpost pointing right.

Your direction is signed "Marshall Meadows, 2½". The path is narrow and the grass is long in summer. On the left the golf course is generally not a problem, but one of the tees straddles the right of way, so let any golfers play off before crossing. Walk along the edge of a cultivated field, then more easily through pastures. The suburbs of Berwick seem to stay with you for ever, but when the industrial estate passes you are free of the town.

the Border Stile.

Your next landmark is the Needle's Eye, a natural archway in the sandstone cliff. A mile further on are the curving cliffs of Marshall Meadows Bay. A ladder stile takes you over the wall to the caravan park. Go right, along the roadway, going uphill and over the stone bridge. Years ago the railway was diverted inland, leaving the bridge behind.

Over the bridge a fingerpost gives an encouraging message, "Scottish Border, ½." Walk round the sea edge of the last English field and climb two stiles into Scotland. Turn left and follow the Border fence to the railway wall and admire the railway signs, which are impossible to read from a train travelling at 100 m.p.h.

Follow the railway boundary wall to the right for half a mile to a bridge crossing the railway. Go through a gate, left, onto a track.

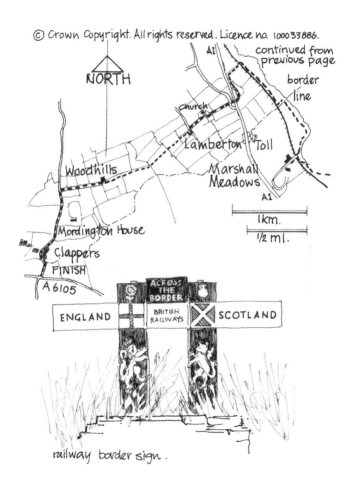

railway border sign.

Leave all gates as you find them.

Follow the stone track up towards the busy A1 road, turning left to come out onto the access road for the A1 overbridge. Pause on the bridge looking south, you will see twin laybys either side of the road, marking the actual Border line at Lamberton Toll. The old toll house disappeared years ago, a victim of road "improvements."

Runaway couples were married there, as at Gretna. A notice in the window read, "Ginger beer sold here and marriages performed!"

Go straight ahead up a narrow road between the remains of whales jawbones, set in stone bases. Just past Lamberton Nurseries is a parking place in front of a grassy mound with all that remains of "the Great Kirk of Lamberton". In 1502 Margaret Tudor came here with a retinue of 2000 to be handed over to the Scottish Commissioners who escorted her to Edinburgh to marry James IV. She was 13 years old and 100 years later her great-grandson crossed the border into England as King of both nations.

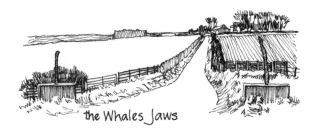

the Whales Jaws

22

the Great Kirk of Lamberton

Continue up the road to a tee junction. Go left
along the road, which is medieval and was the
main road into Scotland until 1820. After a short
distance turn right to a public footpath sign
at double gates. Go through, uphill, to a gate on
the left. In the field follow the fence uphill to a
stile. Be careful to keep clear of electric fences
in this area.

Climb the stile at the top of the field and
keep straight on across the next field to find
another stile. Follow the fence line to a third
stile with a wicket gate just beyond it. The
wire across the top of the stile is not electrified.

You will now find yourself in an avenue of
newly planted hawthorns. To the right is the

Cockit Hat plantation, while away to the left is the Northumbrian coast and ahead the bulk of the Cheviots dominates the skyline.

Follow the hawthorn avenue downhill and at the bottom cross a stile on the right to join the road at Woodhills. The road leads down to meet the Mordington road. Go left and walk down to Clappers with its row of cottages and the old smithy on the corner. Go left past the old school, following the road round to the right. The Border Line comes down a small burn from the left to follow the centre line of the road.

The remains of Mordington Church stand in the graveyard on the right. William de Mordington was Chancellor of Scotland during the reign of Alexander II.

Down at the A6105 the walk finishes. There is a bus shelter on the right with regular buses in to Berwick.

ENGLAND

sign at Mordington crossroads.

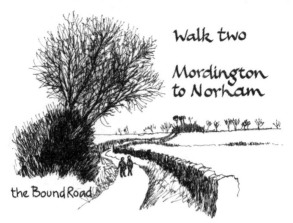

Walk two

Mordington to Norham

the Bound Road

The second walk follows the ancient Bound Road to Whiteadder Water and the River Tweed, which is followed upstream to Horncliffe and Norham. The route is low level and easy walking, but with a few tricky sections of riverbank. It is 9 miles (14·4km) and can be walked in 5-6 hours. Stout footwear is essential. There are regular bus services from Berwick to the start, and back from the finish at Norham.

At Mordington crossroads, cross the road and follow the Bound Road south past the Kirkhill and HighCocklaw road ends. The England/Scotland Border runs down the centre of the road, indicating that the road was in existence before the Border was established.

When you reach the tee junction turn right along the straight road to Edrington Castle Farm. As you go through the farm there is a short stretch of medieval walling,

26

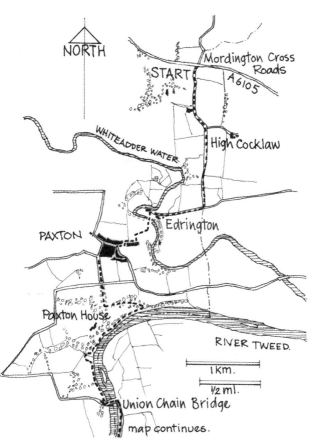

NORTH

Mordington Cross Roads

START

A6105

WHITEADDER WATER

High Cocklaw

PAXTON

Edrington

Paxton House

RIVER TWEED.

1 km.

½ ml.

Union Chain Bridge

map continues.

on the left, which is all that survives of Edrington Castle. Being so close to the Border both nations knocked it about through the years.

Continue downhill towards the Whiteadder, bearing left at the foot of the hill, and passing the old mill. A sign between two windows marks the water level during the great flood of 1948. Cross the footbridge and the steep path to follow a path, straight ahead, alongside the field hedge. Bear left towards the houses, then follow the road, right, turning left then right into Paxton village centre.

Opposite the Cross Inn (refreshments) go down a narrow lane between houses and a high wall, turning to the right. The lane appears to be a dead end, but there is a narrow path on the left, follow this, to the B6460 road, turning left to follow the road down to the cross roads. Cross over and enter the grounds of Paxton House with its Palladian lodges.

Edrington Castle remains

Edrington Mill

At the bottom of the drive, before the bridge, go left and follow a well-formed path through trees round Linn Dean. Down at the River Tweed go right, cross the footbridge and walk along the riverside path, passing the reconstructed boat house. Salmon fishing is still carried on here and, if the tide is right, you might see the fishers at work.

At the end of the grounds the path bends right, uphill. At the first corner go left along a minor path to a footbridge. Turn right, beside the boundary wall and go over a stile in a doorway. MIND YOUR HEAD. Down at the riverside is a stile onto the riverside path, which brings you to Union Chain Bridge. Past the old fishing shiel turn right, uphill, to the road and Chain Bridge.

An information board explains the significance of this historic bridge. Cross the bridge, returning to England at the mid span. The Border follows the centre line of the Tweed to beyond Coldstream, where it turns south to the Cheviots.

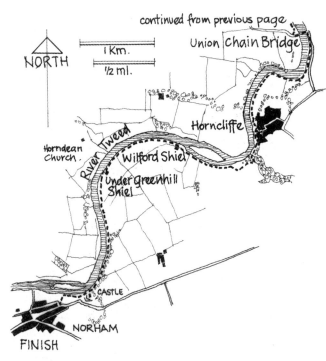

continued from previous page

Union Chain Bridge

NORTH

1 Km.

1/2 ml.

River Tweed

Horndean Church.

Horncliffe

Wilford Shiel

Under Greenhill Shiel

CASTLE

NORHAM

FINISH

Along the river banks beware of Giant Hogweed (HERACLEUM MANTEGAZZIANUM) with large rhubarb-like leaves and 12 ft. (3·6M) high stems and large seed heads. The sap photosensitises the skin causing large, painful water blisters. Keep clear of this plant.

Over the bridge go right, up the road to a fingerpost on the right, "Horncliffe, 1'4," pointing to the tree-lined river path, past a ruined fishing shiel on the Heugh to a pair of wooden buildings. Turn left up the stony track. Towards the top there is a fingerpost on the right pointing up a flight of steps and a kissing gate. The Fishers Arms in Main Street offers refreshments. For the moment carry straight on keeping the playground on the left and as you come to the road keep to the right, past houses, until you reach a fingerpost on the right, "Norham, 3."

Follow the steps down to the river and walk to a narrow footbridge. This is the foot of Horncliffe Glen, "one of the loveliest in this part of the world — It is a deep ravine, woods on one side where the primroses in spring are wonderful, bracken and whin on the other."

P. Anderson Graham.

Horncliffe — path to Norham.

31

below
the walls of
Norham Castle

Climb the steep steps and at the top turn sharp right and follow the path through trees and round the top of the bank on a poor, canted path down to a stile on the left. Cross over the field to a stile in the bottom corner, going left to follow the riverside, passing Wilford Shiel and Upper Greenhill Shiel.

Birdlife is plentiful on this quiet stretch of river, solitary herons, wagtails, mallard, goosander are commonly seen and occasionally Kingfishers. As you reach the end of the fields the path bears left, up into the woods. There are many twists and turns with steps up and down. This wood is subject to slippage every winter and sometimes careful footwork is required.

Ahead you can catch glimpses of Norham Castle peeping above the trees. The prince bishops of Durham built the castle to control two important fords on the Tweed. The first Castle was started in 1121, several burnings and sackings later the final rebuilding was in 1515.

Eventually the wooded path descends to a stile.
Continue along the riverside of the last field to
a footbridge which brings you to the play park.
Cross the park diagonally to arrive in Norham.
Follow the road to the village green, the starting
point of the next walk.

Norham has two pubs, a shop, a butcher,
a baker, a post office and a public convenience.

Coming
in to
Norham

Walk Three
Norham to Cornhill

This is a low-level walk mainly following the River Tweed on its south bank. It is 8 miles (13 km.) and can be walked in 4 or 5 hours. The terrain can be uneven in places and muddy in wet weather, so boots are recommended. There is public transport at both ends of the walk and shops and refreshments in Norham and Cornhill.

The walk starts from Norham green, with its village cross. The stepped base is medieval. At the south-west corner of the green there is a finger post "Ladykirk Bridge / Twizel Bridge." This leads almost immediately to the gates of St. Cuthbert's Parish Church, where another fingerpost points to the River Tweed. The path goes through the churchyard on a grass path, passing to the right of the church.

It is worthwhile taking time to view the south elevation of the chancel, to the left.

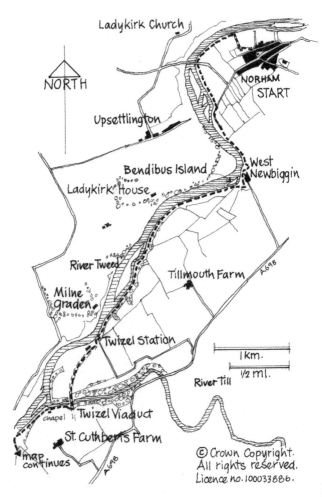

Ladykirk Church

NORTH

Upsettlington

Bendibus Island

Ladykirk House

River Tweed

Milne Graden

Twizel Station

chapel

Twizel Viaduct

St. Cuthbert's Farm

map continues

A698

NORHAM START

West Newbiggin

Tillmouth Farm

A698

River Till

1 km.

½ ml.

© Crown Copyright.
All rights reserved.
Licence no. 100033886.

36

DETAIL OF THE CHANCEL, NORHAM CHURCH.

The Norman windows are virtually original. Edward I met the Scottish nobles in the church to arbitrate on John Baliol's claim to the throne.

Continue on the path to the right of the church going right over a stone stile to reach the river bank. On reaching the river turn left (upstream) to the Ladykirk & Norham bridge. The path passes below the bridge, forking left up to a stile. Cross the stile and go right along the field edge. A well-maintained fishing shiel comes into view on the opposite bank where the river meanders.

Shortly after crossing another stile the path forks again. Take the left path which arrives at a wicket gate on to a lane opposite farm buildings. Turn right along the lane, heading for a prominent white house. At the house gates (the Columns) ignore a fingerpost to the left and go through the gate straight ahead into a field by the river. In the woodland ahead there is a convenient riverside bench directly opposite another fishing shiel on the Scottish side.

At a path junction at the foot of Newbiggin Dean bear right to cross a foot bridge over the stream (the left fork leads up the Dean). Heading back to the riverside, look behind you up the Dean and you may glimpse the Newbiggin railway viaduct.

Shortly afterwards look out for steps on the right leading down to the riverbank and a fingerpost, "Twizel Bridge." As the path regains the riverside notice the small island in the river. It is curiously named Bendibus Island.

The path continues past another stone-built fishing shiel, this time on the English side. On the opposite bank of the river Ladykirk House comes into view. It is relatively modern, the original house having been demolished. The path next enters woodland at a point opposite a neat round fishing shiel. Soon you reach a point where the Tweed comes in round both sides of Kippie Island. Take great care here, as the path is eroded close to the river.

foot of Newbiggin Dean

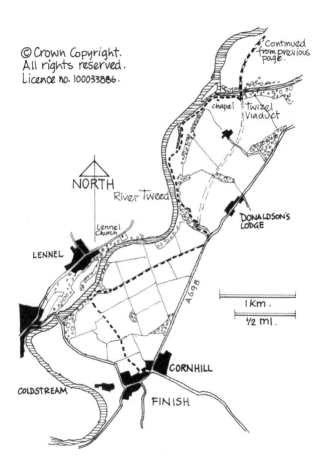

Continued from previous page.

chapel   Twizel Viaduct

NORTH

River Tweed

Lennel Church

DONALDSON'S LODGE

LENNEL

A698

1 Km.

½ ml.

CORNHILL

COLDSTREAM

FINISH

39

After half a mile, listen out for the sound of the river rushing over a weir at the point where the river splits at the upstream end of Dreeper Island. This is just below the imposing Milne Graden House on the Scottish bank. It is a neoclassical mansion, built in 1822. The path ascends the river bank and the view upstream opens out. This is a good place for a short break.

At the top of the bank the path passes behind a house to reach a track and finger posts. Ignore the route to "Twizel Bridge," but instead follow the sign "Permissive Path, Twizel Viaduct and Tweed Riverside Path." You are now on the course of the old Tweedmouth-Kelso railway. On the left and right are the staggered platforms of Twizel station, still easily visible beneath thick vegetation. The summer 1952 timetable showed Twizell (then spelt with two Ls), as being served by four trains per day in each direction.

Follow the track bed all the way to the viaduct.
Twizel viaduct is an imposing grade II listed stone
structure spanning the River Till. It was built
in 1849 and in use for passenger and goods trains
until the mid 1960s. In 2005 it was made into
an official footpath. Pause at the mid point to
take in the views of the peaceful river.
An old rhyme compares the Tweed and Till,

> "Tweed says to Till,
> 'what gars ye rin sae still?'
> says Till to Tweed,
> 'though ye run wi' speed,
> And I rin slaw,
> Whaur ye droon ae man,
> I droon twa.' "

River Till from the viaduct

St. Cuthbert's Chapel

Descend the steps on the right at the far end of the viaduct and cross the stile down at the riverside. Continue past the remains of St. Cuthbert's Chapel to the confluence of the rivers Till and Tweed. After passing through a gate continue along a track leading shortly to an open stretch beside the "Great Haugh." Just before entering more woodland there is a welcome riverside bench offering a further rest.

The path now climbs Callerheugh Bank to a ladder stile, then turns right along a field edge. The course of the old railway is again reached and followed for a few yards by turning right over a stile. Ahead of you can be seen a railway bridge, but it cannot be reached because the right of way turns left along a track to reach the main road. Turn right along the road, but after just over a minute turn off to the right at a fingerpost "Coldstream Bridge." The path now passes through fields back to the Tweed.

On the Scottish side of the river can be seen Lennel churchyard. Within the graveyard are the remains of the medieval church of St. Mary which is associated with the nuns of Coldstream Priory. For many years there was a ferry across to Lennel.

As the path nears the river cross the stile on your right to reach the point at which Cornhill Castle used to stand. There are no visible remains. As the path continues through woodland high above the river, look for a ladder stile on your left. Cross the stile and follow the hedgerow directly towards Cornhill, entering the village through a farmyard.

Buses back to the start at Norham depart from the Collingwood Arms: Munro's route, 67 (weekdays), or 223 (Sundays).

approaching Cornhill.

Walk Four
Cornhill to Kirk Yetholm

This walk of 11 miles (17.5km.) follows the Border, first in England, then on the Border and finally in Scotland. Leaving the centre line of the Tweed, the Border crosses low lying farmland to the Cheviots. This border plain was much disputed through the centuries and many official inspections and surveys are recorded in the 15th, 16th and 17th centuries.

"The common entree and passage of the Scottes for invadynge this realm or makinge any spoyle in tyme of warr." Bowes survey, 1542.

The enclosures of the 18th century finally formalised the situation.

The first section is along the old Berwick-Kelso railway line and is easy to follow. The middle section is largely on quiet country lanes. The final section follows an old track from Hoselaw to Yetholm, mostly on clear paths, some muddy.

From the roundabout at the east end of Cornhill, take the A697 road towards Wooler (SE)

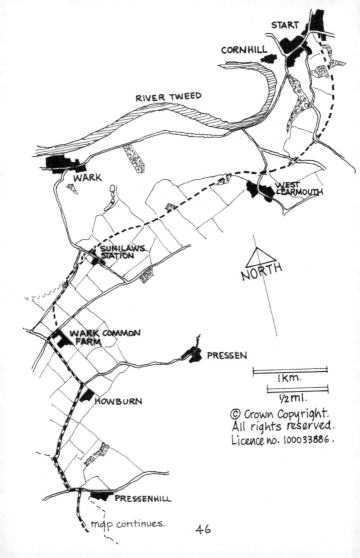

START

CORNHILL

RIVER TWEED

WARK

WEST LEARMOUTH

SUNILAWS STATION

NORTH

WARK COMMON FARM

PRESSEN

1km.

½ml.

© Crown Copyright.
All rights reserved.
Licence no. 100033886.

HOWBURN

PRESSENHILL

map continues.

46

for 150 yards to the line of the old railway. A waymarked path on the right side of the road(s) leads up steps to the old railway line, which is followed for three and a half miles to just past Sunilaws Station. Ignore the waymarked path to the left in half a mile.

From the higher parts of the line, particularly the two viaducts, there are good views of the Tweed and Coldstream, where General Monk raised the Coldstream Guards in 1659. Further on, Wark Castle, by the river, is now a grassy mound; it guarded two important fords.

"Wark's history, from the twelfth down to at least the sixteenth century, is perhaps without parallel for surprises, assaults, sieges, blockades, surrenders, evacuations, burnings, restorations, slaughters." (Denham Tracts). No wonder it's just a grassy mound.

Here is the last glimpse of the Tweed, our companion for so long. Just past West Learmouth the railway line ceases to be a right of way and is now a permissive route. At this point there is a waymark post.

approaching Wark Common

the Tin Tabernacle at Howburn.

Ignore the diagonally crossing track and keep to
the railway line. At Sunilaws Station a minor road
crosses the track. Keep ahead, taking the farm
track just to the left of the old line, thus avoiding
the front of the cottages. It quickly rejoins the
line. In 250 yards the line crosses a minor
road by a bridge. The route leaves the railway
line 200 yards after, just before a small
plantation on the left. There is a clear path
down to the road on your left (GR 822371).

Go right (SW) along the road for 300 yards
where there is a signposted path on the left at
a small gate. The path goes across the field,
which is usually cropped, following the
direction of the fingerpost to the left hand
end of the buildings at Wark Common. The
large field is registered common land, presumably
a remnant from the enclosures of the 18th
century.

Here, on joining the road, turn right (W) to
cross roads. Turn left (S) on the road to Howburn
and Pressen Hill.

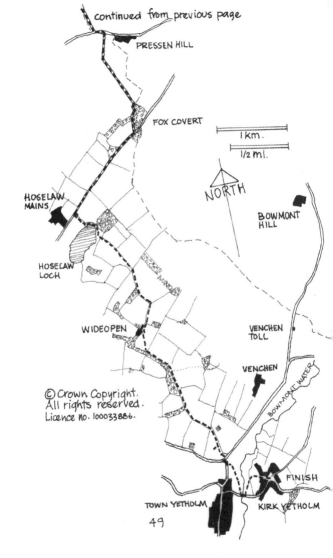

continued from previous page

PRESSEN HILL

FOX COVERT

1 km.

1/2 ml.

NORTH

HOSELAW
MAINS

BOWMONT
HILL

HOSELAW
LOCH

WIDEOPEN

VENCHEN
TOLL

VENCHEN

BOWMONT WATER

FINISH

TOWN YETHOLM

KIRK YETHOLM

At the T junction at Howburn turn right.

At the second track into the farm is a disused Tin Tabernacle. In just over half a mile at a sharp bend the Border Line joins the road and follows it to the tee junction. Here turn left (E) for 100 yards and take the road to the right (S).

The farm on the left is Pressen Hill, where the Border Line runs up the farm road, so that the farmer lives in England and parks his car in Scotland.

The road climbs steadily uphill to a wood, Fox Covert, and at it, just touches the Border. The Border has never been marked through the wood – the line on the map is notional – and Fox Covert was formerly called No Man's Land. At the end of the wood, go right (SW) towards Hoselaw, a mile away.

At the first house on the left, take the track left (SE) down to Hoselaw Loch. Follow the track round the east end of the loch to a gate across the track about 100 yards beyond the end. This can be very wet and muddy.

Pressen Hill

Hoselaw Loch

Go through the gate and turn sharp left (SE) up the side of the wall to another gate. The track ahead is clear, following fence lines. It goes down into a dip where it changes to a southerly direction and goes uphill to the ridge ahead, passing a wood on the right.

On reaching the ridge and a tee junction go right (SW) to Wideopen. Up here on the higher ground skylarks sing overhead. Take the track from the farm to a wood, the edge of which it now follows. In about 600 yards the farm track veers off left away from the corner of the wood. Turn right off the track (S) at this point, following the edge of the wood. Initially no path is obvious and it would be easy to miss the turn, the route continues along the side of the wood, over the shoulder of Venchen Hill. It goes through a gateway in a stone wall.

From here the Cheviot Hills ahead beckon, with the next section along the Border in view. Town Yetholm nestles in the valley, Kirk Yetholm is still hidden.

The track goes downhill towards Yetholm, with a stone wall on your right. It comes down to a corner and there is a gate into the field below. This field, usually grazed by cattle, is boggy in places and it is best to take a line well to the right of the wall, but making for the ruin of Braehouse. A better track is joined to the left of the ruin and goes down to the road. The remains of Virtue Well is in some trees just before the gate.

On reaching the road, go right and in 100 metres ignore the road on the right to Kelso. Instead cross the small bridge, then go through a gate into the field on the left. Here, skirting the school on your right, make for the bridge over Bowmont Water ahead. Go over a stile onto the road, cross the bridge and immediately go into the field on your left, signposted St. Cuthbert's Way.

Braehouse

Follow a clear path to Kirk Yetholm Green, passing the Youth Hostel. Kirk Yetholm was famously the home of the Border gipsies and is the end of the Pennine Way.

There are bus services to both Cornhill and Yetholm. There are hotels in Cornhill, Town Yetholm and Kirk Yetholm as well as other accommodation. Kirk Yetholm has an SYHA hostel. There are no facilities of any kind en route.

Kirk Yetholm Green

Kirk Yetholm to Cocklawfoot
walk five

"the land in God's own holding, bounded by the line where the shepherd's crook supplants the plough." Abel Chapman

This is the most strenuous section of the walk. The route follows the Border Ridge and crosses the shoulder of Cheviot. It is a serious hill walk, requiring proper equipment and experience, including map reading and compass skills. It is necessary to use a map, preferably 1:25,000 scale. An easier alternative, in case of poor weather, or if preferred, is given. Even this reaches a height of 500 metres, and is only waymarked initially.

THE MAIN ROUTE.

It is 13.5 miles (21.6 km) from Kirk Yetholm to Cocklawfoot and there is an ascent in the region of 930 metres. The route follows the

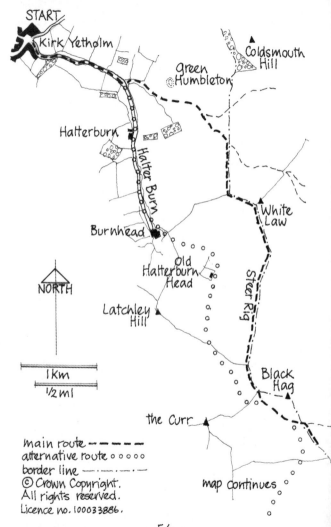

START

Kirk Yetholm

Coldsmouth Hill

Green Humbleton

Halterburn

Halter Burn

White Law

Burnhead

Old Halterburn Head

Steer Rig

NORTH

Latchley Hill

1 Km

1/2 ml

Black Hag

the Curr

main route - - - - - -
alternative route o o o o o
border line - · - · - · -
© Crown Copyright.
All rights reserved.
Licence no. 100033886.

map continues

56

Pennine Way and after two miles the Border, until it drops down to Cocklawfoot at Hexpethgate (not named on maps). It is a superb walk with extensive views across the Borders and North Northumberland. There is no dwelling after leaving KirkYetholm until Cocklawfoot; your companions are the birds, animals and plants of the hills. Yet there is much of historic interest from prehistory to the days of the Reivers.

At Kirk Yetholm Green take the road uphill, initially south. The board marking the end of the Pennine Way (PW) is at the start, and the PW is waymarked throughout. At this point St. Cuthbert's Way shares the route. Just before leaving the village we pass the Gipsy Palace, a small cottage, once home of the King of the Border Gipsies. The road climbs steeply and then drops down to the Halterburn valley. At the foot of the hill, by a small wood, (GR839 279) there is a parking area

the Gipsy Palace.

the Stob Stanes

and if using a vehicle it is possible to start from
here. Leaving the road, there is a small footbridge
a little above the ford. Go back to the ford and
pick up the PW going uphill on a rising,
contouring path. In just under a mile, at
G.R. 850 272, St. Cuthbert's Way goes off to the
left at a signpost. Keep on the PW, which
reaches the Border wall in 500 yards; Before
this the Stob Stanes can be visited on the right
of the path, leaving just before a small knowe.
One stone is standing, the other fallen. The Border
fence is now followed for just over ten miles,
making route finding very straightforward.

The first hill is White Law. After a short descent
there is a long gradual climb up Steer Rig to the
shoulder of Black Hag. The path stays in Scotland.
Down on the right are the ruins of Old Halterburnhead
and clear signs of an ancient settlement, on the left
is the valley of the Trowup Burn. Just below
Black Hag the alternative route joins us at a signpost (G.R. 858 236). At this point the path briefly

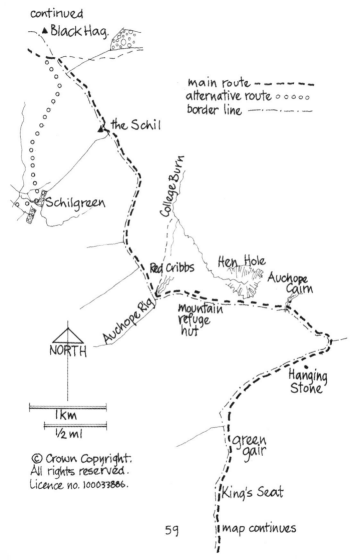

continued

▲ Black Hag.

the Schil ▲

College Burn

Schilgreen

main route — — —
alternative route ○ ○ ○ ○ ○
border line —·—·—·—

Red Cribbs

Hen Hole

Auchope Cairn

mountain refuge hut

Auchope Rig

NORTH

1 km

½ ml

© Crown Copyright.
All rights reserved.
Licence no. 100033886.

Hanging Stone

green gair

King's Seat

map continues

leaves the Border to avoid the summit of Black Hag. The alternative path leaves our route in 400 yards (G.R. 861 233). There is no waymark for this escape route, which will be useful if the weather changes.

The P W rejoins the Border wall, goes through to the English side and climbs steeply to the Schil. The summit tor is in Scotland, with excellent views all round. The lovely College Valley lies to the north east. South east, on the Cheviot, is the rocky chasm of the Henhole. The path drops south along the ridge for one-and-a-half miles to the head of College Valley at Red Cribbs (G.R. 874 201). This area was a meeting point for the Wardens of the Eastern March up to the sixteenth century.

Here the Auchope Rig runs south west, offering another escape route. It is not waymarked, but go through the gate and follow the track with the fence on ones left until the col between Auchope Rig and Bonnie Laws (G.R. 859 195), where the alternative route is joined.

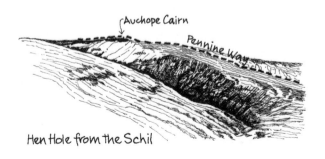

Hen Hole from the Schil

the Hanging Stane.

Our path continues on the P.W. and turns east. Uniquely, for the next mile-and-a-half, Scotland is to the south and England to the north! Ahead, after the mountain refuge hut, is the steep ascent to the Auchope Cairn, with HenHole falling away on the left, a grand mountain scene. It is said that Lochnagar and the Grampian Mountains are visible in really clear winter weather. There follows a section on boardwalks. The terrain is typical of the summit of the Cheviot. In 700 yards at the junction of three fences (with signpost), our route turns west. The other path goes to the summit of Cheviot, 815 metres, the highest point in the Borough and indeed Northumberland and the Eastern Borders. It is a possible diversion of nearly 2.5 miles.

The path now descends to the southwest. Where the descent steepens a diversion of 100 yards can be made to the Hanging Stane (G.R. 892 190). It is not obvious from the path, but is quickly seen.

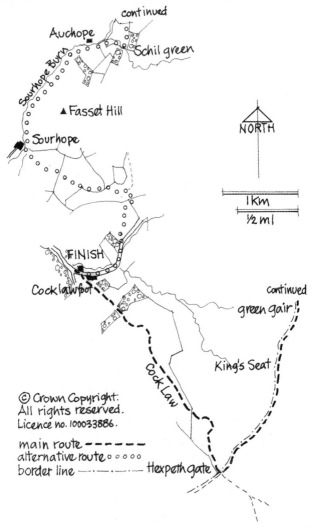

continued

Auchope

Schil green

Sourhope Burn

▲ Fasset Hill

Sourhope

NORTH

1 Km

½ ml

FINISH

Cocklawfoot

continued

green gair

King's Seat

Cock Law

main route   – – – – –
alternative route   ○ ○ ○ ○ ○
border line   –··–··–

Hexpeth gate

It marked the boundary of the Eastern and Middle Marches and is a rocky outcrop. The path follows the P.W. for three-and-a-half miles, often on stone slabs brought from Lancashire cotton mills to make it easier to cross the bogs. We leave the P.W. and the Border Ridge at the Hexpath gate, not named on maps (G.R. 871 160). There is a fingerpost and an obvious track crosses the Border, going north to Cocklawfoot and southwest to Uswayford. You will return to this point to start the next section.

For Cocklawfoot go right. The track is always clear on the ground, eventually passing through a plantation and continuing down to the farm in just over two miles. Beyond the farm (left) is a ford and a bridge across Kelsocleugh Burn. The bridge is not suitable for vehicles but can be crossed on foot. It leads to a parking area and the end of this section.

For Uswayford, go left at Hexpathgate. Ignore the Salters Road sign and take the next path on the left signed Uswayford. The farm is 1½ miles from the ridge.

Hexpathgate

THE ALTERNATIVE ROUTE.

The route is 9 miles from Kirk Yetholm to Cocklawfoot. It mostly follows valleys, crossing a couple of cols and is largely on clear tracks, though, apart from the initial stretch, is not waymarked. It is necessary to use a map, preferably 1:25000 scale. The route is in Scotland throughout.

Follow the main route to the Halterburn valley (G.R. 839 276). Follow the road up the valley, passing Halterburn farm on your right. This is the low level option of the Pennine Way. In about one mile the road crosses the burn as it approaches Burnhead farm. Look out for the waymarked path on your left. It crosses the fence by a stile and continues up the side of the fence, with Burnhead on the other bank of the burn. After passing the farm it drops to a footbridge and goes up the opposite bank to join a farm track. This diversion is not on older O.S. maps. Continue, initially east then south on the track. In about half-a-mile we reach the ruins of Old Halterburnhead — a good picnic stop. The path is now grassy, making its way to the valley head at Pipers Faulds (G.R. 851 243).

approaching Burnhead

Old
Halterburnhead

Go through the gate and take the track on the left which climbs in a zig zag to reach the col between the Curr and Black Hag. Shortly after the Pennine Way is joined at G.R.858 236. In 400 yards (G.R.861 233), shortly before the wall ahead (the Border), take the track to the right,(SE). It is not very clear at first. Initially it contours round the head of the valley of the Rowhope Burn before dropping steeply to it. Now a clear track, it follows the burn south. The track divides just after a plantation and after crossing the Alderhope Burn.

Go right, passing Auchope on the other side of the burn and continue round Fasset Hill. You will see Sourhope, the hillfarming research station, below. At the track junction take the track right, down to Sourhope. Just after passing a row of cottages on your left. take the track to your left to cross the bridge over Kaim Burn and continue on past the black barn in a southeasterly direction. The track gradually climbs along the side of Park Law. Cashmere goats are often seen in this vicinity. In about a mile from Sourhope, at G.R.859 196, take a faint quad bike track right, S, up to the col between Auchope Rig and

Bonnie Laws, to meet the fence coming down the Rig. Go right and then through the gate on your left and immediately through the gate in front of you. The Track now drops down slightly east of south, To cross the small burn on your left at a vehicle bridge and then down the east side of Cheviot Burn. It is not shown on the map. It soon reaches Cocklawfoot, coming in through the farm buildings.

There are no facilities of any kind after leaving Kirk Yetholm. There is no public transport to Cocklawfoot and a car or pre-arranged taxi will be necessary. Mobile phone reception is extremely limited in the Cheviots, so do not rely on this in making any arrangements.

If you are doing a continuous walk it is possible to arrange accommodation at Uswayford Farm. Follow the main route turning left at the Hexpath Gate and dropping down to Uswayford. Next morning take the path north from Uswayford to join Salter's Road at GR886155. The public road does not go to Uswayford.

Walk six
Cocklawfoot to Hartside

The Borough boundary which we are following now leaves the national border and makes its way through the Cheviots in an easterly direction. Luckily there are ancient tracks, Clennell Street and Salter's Road, which shadow the boundary. There are no facilities en route and no escape routes, so take everything you will need, especially wet weather gear.

The walk is 11·25 miles (18km) and it will take about 7 hours. There is no public transport at either end of the walk. Map reading and compass work will be required, so do not attempt this walk unless you are experienced in navigation. Check the weather forecast and be prepared for sudden changes in the weather.

There is parking on the roadside before Cocklawfoot Farm. Cross the plank bridge and go through a gate into the farmyard. A fingerpost on the right, marked Border Ridge, indicates your route. This is Clennell Street

START
Cocklawfoot

Fort

Settlement

Cock Law

The Bank

Outer Cock Law

Border Fence
Pennine Way

Hexpath Gate

Davidsons Linn

map continues below.

continued

Davidsons Linn

Salter's Road

Lint Langs

Broad Hill

ford

ford

ford

ford

ford

Hen Hill

map continues

which leads to Alwinton in the Coquet valley.
The track ahead is clear. It passes through
a stand of trees (last chance for a discreet
pee stop), before gradually climbing over Cock
Law. This is a good vantage point to view
the broad sweep of the Border Ridge from
Windy Gyle (right) to the Cheviot and the Schill (left).
Go through a gate and follow the track as it
veers left round Outer Cock Law. Note the deep
furrows on the right, worn by the many hooves
of horses and cattle through the ages.

The next gate is Hexpathgate, on the English/
Scottish border. Once through you cross the
Pennine Way, but your route goes straight
ahead. Hexpathgate was a meeting place for
Wardens of the Border Marches on truce days.
It was hereabouts that Lord Francis Russell was
murdered at one such meeting. He was the
son-in-law of Sir John Forster, warden of the
middle marches.

Follow the track, still Clennell Street, gently
down hill. The first fingerpost on the left directs
you along Salter's Road, but at present it is
impassable through the trees due to irresponsible
scrambling motorcyclists who have churned the
peat into evil black porridge. You are strongly
advised to continue on to a second fingerpost
200 yards further on, signed Uswayford.

The path leads down into the trees on a
muddy ride. On reaching a forest track go left,
looking out for a waymark on the right. Go a
short distance beyond it and take an easier way
into the trees, over a plank bridge. You are now
on Salter's Road. Care needs to be taken for the
way is narrow, with deep ruts and steep sides
with slippery tree roots.

Eventually you come out of the trees on the
side of the steep valley of the Usway Burn.
Below you is the picturesque waterfall of
Davidson's Linn — a good picnic spot. Further
upstream a new footbridge takes you over the
burn.

waterfall at
Davidson's Linn

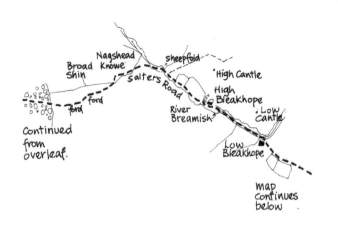

Nagshead Knowe

Broad Shin

Salters Road

sheepfold

High Cantle

High Breakhope

River Breamish

Low Cantle

Low Breakhope

ford

ford

ford

Continued from overleaf.

map continues below.

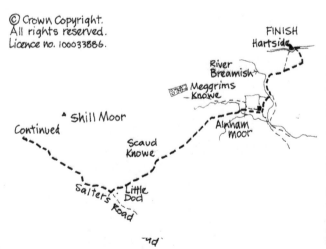

FINISH
Hartside

River Breamish

Meggrims Knowe

▲ Shill Moor

Continued

Scaud Knowe

Alnham moor

Salters Road

Little Dod

ᵈ

72

looking Back to High Bleakhope

Go right on a path climbing towards more
trees, where it widens into a track. More ruts
and bogs greet you as you make your way
along to another fingerpost showing Salter's
Road to the left. Be careful here because
it would be all too easy to continue along
the forest ride which takes you to the right.
Keep on the left hand track until it emerges
from the trees at a gate.

Out in the open the way is less clear as
it descends to the Bleakhopes. It is advisable
to take compass bearings to get you downhill
to the infant River Breamish. When you reach
a gated fence on your left, go through and
continue down towards a sheep stell and the
river. Follow downstream towards High
Bleakhope and walk through the farm, where
the way becomes a metalled road.

In the 12th century the Cistercian monks of
Newminster were granted huge areas of these
hills for sheep grazing by the de Umfraville lords
of Redesdale and Harbottle. They shepherded sheep
here until the dissolution of the monasteries.

Low
Bleakhope

Walk on to Low Bleakhope and, where the road
bends left, continue straight on through a shallow
ford and steadily uphill. The stony path is still
Salter's Road and it leads through a gate to the
crest of a hill. The path descends and ahead of you
another small hill, Little Dod, can be seen. As you
approach it take the waymarked post on the left,
directing you down to Alnhammoor Farm and
away from Salter's Road.

At the bottom of the valley the Shank Burn
appears on the right and the path crosses a
small side stream to a steep stile. Veer right
with the path past the farmhouse, then sharp
left through a small field with wicket gates
at either end. Coming onto the road go right,
downhill and cross over the River Breamish by
the plank bridge. Turn left and stay on the
road all the way to Hartside.

Alnhammoor

walk seven
Hartside to
Powburn

heading up to Cobden

This walk takes you from the high Cheviots down through the foothills to the lowlands. It also takes you from the Bronze and Iron Ages to the Roman occupation. You start in an area of sporadic settlement, with stone foundations of clustered huts and traces of early cultivation on the hillsides. Later the foothills have hillforts, built by incoming Celtic peoples and finally you arrive at Powburn where the A697 road overlies the Devil's Causeway, a Roman Road.

The route is hilly, but with moderate inclines. It is 8.6 miles (13.7 km.) and can be walked in about 4 or 5 hours. There are permanent wet, muddy places, so stout footwear is recommended. Hartside has no public transport, but Powburn is on a main bus route.

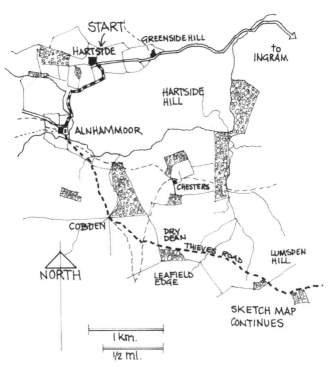

START

HARTSIDE

GREENSIDE HILL

to INGRAM

HARTSIDE HILL

ALNHAMMOOR

CHESTERS

COBDEN

DRY DEAN

THIEVES ROAD

LUMSDEN HILL

LEAFIELD EDGE

SKETCH MAP CONTINUES

NORTH

1 km.

½ ml.

Cobden

From the road junction, just before Hartside, take the metalled road South, finger-post-Alnham Moor-1/2, down to the River Breamish and Alnhammoor just beyond. Hartside Hill, which you pass on the left, has traces of early homesteads and there are rig and furrow traces to the north of Alnhammoor.

About 200 yards after crossing the river and at the top of a rise, just before the farm buildings, are two small wooden gates, with waymarks, either side of a small field. From the second gate bear left and shortly pass through a metal farm-gate before crossing over the Shank Burn by a wooden bridge to a stile and a second metal farm-gate into a riverside meadow.

Cross the meadow, bearing right, making

for a waymarked stile and a wooden farm-gate onto a well-defined track rising beyond. Continue heading uphill on the rutted track keeping the fence on the left for part of the way to the corner of a wood on the skyline at Cobden. At the wood cross the Cobden Burn at the ford to the waymarked stile next to a wooden farm-gate.

From Cobden continue uphill on a waymarked grassy track across the moors, making for a line of trees on the horizon and a metal farm-gate situated at the start of the Thieves Road. The Border troubles would appear to have given rise to this name, as reivers would use it as a quick route for their "lifted" stock back over the Border. The Thieves Road connects with Salter's Road. Many of the Border Streets were also used as trading routes, but they probably initially connected Celtic settlements on either side of the Border Ridge.

Whilst heading eastwards along the grassy track of Thieves Road, between Leafield Edge and Dry Dean, excellent views can be seen of the surrounding hills, including Hedgehope and the Cheviot. Eventually, after crossing a small burn and passing through a couple of metal farm-gates the Thieves Road Plantation is reached. From here head gently downhill to pass through a metal farm-gate, then immediately climb the stile on the left before continuing downhill eastwards, making for the corner of a plantation about 200 yards ahead.

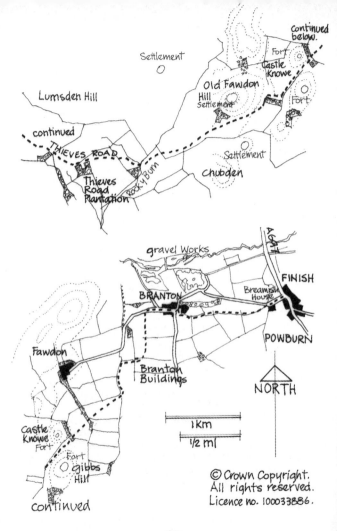

Settlement

Lumsden Hill

continued

THIEVES ROAD

Thieves Road Plantation

Rocky Burn

continued below.

Fort

Castle Knowe

Old Fawdon Hill Settlement

Fort

Settlement

Chubden

gravel Works

A 697

BRANTON

Breamish House

FINISH

Fawdon

Branton Buildings

POWBURN

Castle Knowe Fort

Fort gibbs Hill

continued

NORTH

1 km

1/2 ml

© Crown Copyright.
All rights reserved.
Licence no. 100033886.

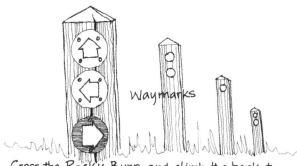

Waymarks

Cross the Rocky Burn and climb the bank to
pass through a metal farm gate, then immediately
turn left and go through a second metal gate to
head uphill across the meadow to a waymarked
wooden gate. The grassy footpath is well defined
and waymarked as it goes up round the north
side of Chubden Hill and over moorland. In summer
and autumn the path can become less obvious when
bracken is waist high. It is then best to head for the
'Y' shaped plantation just before Old Fawdon Hill.
The area in front of this plantation is often running
in water and boggy, the path is not very obvious.

A clearly defined settlement can be seen on
the right and there are hill-top forts on Old Fawdon
Hill, Gibbs Hill and Castle Knowe.

After about 600 yards a rectangular plantation
is reached through which, according to the O.S. map,
the footpath to Branton passes, but it is
indistinguishable in the trees. At present an
alternative route goes through a metal farm-gate
into a field at the left-hand corner of the wood,

waymarked "recommended path". Cross the field to the far gate avoiding a wet area by keeping near the wood until well past, then go back on to the track, a right of way.

This waymarked track passes between Gibbs Hill and Castle Knowe to a gap in a narrow woodland strip and a farm gate, which is often surrounded in mud.

From the top of the rise in the next field make for a gap in a second woodland strip directly ahead. Once through the wood and over the road leading right to Clinch, enter the field opposite and head downhill to the stile in the bottom left-hand corner of the field. Then cross a second stile into the next field. Turn left and, keeping the fence on the left, contour round Dun's Knowe, on the right, to a double metal farm-gate and out onto the drive leading up to Branton Buildings on the right.

Just before the buildings, at the top of the drive, go through two farm gates on the left and follow the waymarked route round behind the north side of Branton Buildings, bearing left to a fence ahead.

farm entrance, Branton.

this way

82

gate protruding from the hedge

Keeping the fence on the right, head north through two fields and a small wooden gate, past the low rise of Cow Hill, to reach a wooden gate just before dropping down to the road. Finger post pointing back – Clinch 1, great Ryle 2½.

Once on the road head east through Branton village to a wide farmyard entrance directly ahead, on a bend. Ignore the right-hand turning to Glanton. Following the direction indicated by the fingerpost on the left enter the farmyard, turning immediately to the right, heading for a wooden farm-gate into a small field. In the field bear left immediately, keeping the house and a stone wall on the left and make for a waymarked stile into the next field.

After a short distance go through a metal farm-gate into the next field heading for a metal gate protruding from the hedge line. Keep heading eastwards, but now with the fence on the right.

Ignoring a footpath to the left, make for the next gate ahead and follow the distinct grassy track down to a gate and on to the road by Breamish House. Fingerpost pointing back - Branton East Side and the Clinch.

A short distance up the road brings you to the A 697 and Powburn. It also lands you on the line of the Devil's Causeway, a Roman road which branches off from Dere Street at Hadrian's Wall and heads north, east of the Cheviots, heading for the mouth of the Tweed.

Powburn is a village with all amenities.

Walk eight Powburn to Ellingham

Coming through Beanley

Having wound its way over the Cheviots the Borough boundary continues eastwards to the sea. Walk eight takes you over the Sandstone Ridge which divides the low lying land at the foot of the Cheviots from the coastal plain.

It is 12 miles (19 km) of easy walking and should take 6 or 7 hours. There are facilities at the start and finish, but nothing in between. If the weather turns really foul there are two escape routes.

Start on the north side of the bridge, opposite the unsigned road (where walk seven finished) and take the public footpath which follows the Pow Burn and woodland edge. (Kingfisher seen here.) On reaching the road to Beanley turn right and walk on for about 1/4 mile to a gate and fingerpost on the left, marked Low Hedgeley. The gravel pits on your left are being landscaped into lakes with islands and are already attracting many species of water birds.

Go through the gate and follow a clear track which skirts round the left edge of a wood, through another gate, ignoring the DEFRA path on your left. At the next gate turn right and follow the fence to a small burn. Cross the burn through the ford or over the log bridge and continue uphill, passing through a gate with Gamekeeper's Cottage on your right.

map continues

Harehope Farm

B6346

Great Wood

Gamekeeper's Cottage

Beanley

A697

Hedgeley Hall

Powburn

START

Keep on the track and up to the road. Turn left and continue along the road through Beanley until you reach a bend with a finger-post on the left signed Eglingham Cottage 1¼. Take this footpath, keeping the fence on your left and passing through a gate

87

until you reach a waymarked gate in the fence. Go through and cross the corner of the field diagonally, over a small burn, to a stile. Keep in the same direction, passing through some hawthorn trees and up to a fence. There is no obvious track here and the ground can be boggy. Follow the direction of the marker, keeping the fence on your right, to a gate. (Look out for deer.) The path here can get very overgrown in summer. Pass through the gate, turn immediately left and through another gate into the Great Wood and its magnificent old beech trees. At the end of the path through the wood turn right through a gate and follow the track to the end of the trees. Here, go half left and take the footpath across the field to a stile in the fence opposite. Cross over and walk through the trees to another stile. Over this turn right and go on to a gate which brings you out onto the Eglingham Road (B6346)

leaving Harehope Farm.

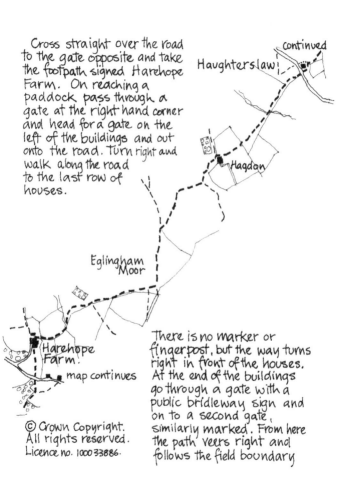

Cross straight over the road to the gate opposite and take the footpath signed Harehope Farm. On reaching a paddock pass through a gate at the right hand corner and head for a gate on the left of the buildings and out onto the road. Turn right and walk along the road to the last row of houses.

Haughterslaw

continued

Hagdon

Eglingham Moor

Harehope Farm

map continues

There is no marker or fingerpost, but the way turns right in front of the houses. At the end of the buildings go through a gate with a public bridleway sign and on to a second gate, similarly marked. From here the path veers right and follows the field boundary

89

to a footbridge with another gate beyond. (Entering access land here.) The path is quite clear, going left before bending right through gorse bushes and bringing you to a small plantation on your left. At a large boulder on the left turn half right towards a wall and walk parallel to it up to Eglingham Moor. Continue until you reach a broad farm track signed Quarry House 2½m. Turn left onto the track. You are now on the Sandstone Ridge. The gently rolling heather moorland overlies fell sandstone, which has provided building material for many of the houses in the Borough.

On reaching a cattle grid ignore the bridle path on the left and continue on the stony track, going right, till you reach the farm at Hagdon. Immediately before the buildings turn left and make your way round to a stile. Cross this and keeping a fence on your right walk away from the farm.

Haughterslaw

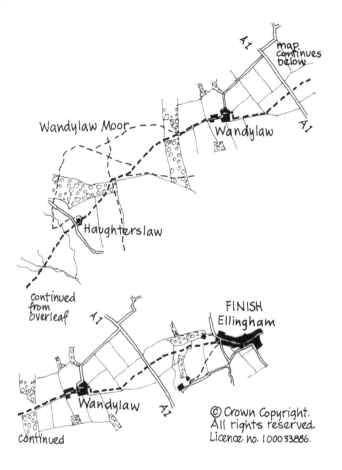

A1

map
continues
below

Wandylaw Moor

Wandylaw

A1

Haughterslaw

continued
from
overleaf

A1

FINISH
Ellingham

Wandylaw

A1

Continued

approaching Wandylaw

Pass through a gate following a line of telegraph poles and cross over a small stream as you approach Haughterslaw, which you can see in the distance.

On reaching the road from North Charlton turn left and walk on a few yards to a bridleway on the right, signed Wandylaw 1½ m. Follow this past the buildings to a gate. Once through go half right to another gate and continue on to a third by some gorse bushes.

(A diversion is planned at Haughterslaw as follows. Continue on the road past the farm to a gate on the right, beyond the last building. Go through and alongside the building, following the track to another gate by the gorse bushes. The diversion will be well marked.)

Keeping the gorse bushes on your left go up to a wood. Enter the wood and on emerging at the other end turn half right to pick up a track which heads to the left of another wood, which can be seen on the skyline.

At a gate follow the direction of the marker arrow onto a track which leads to a gap between two blocks of woodland. For a short way the path immediately after the gate is indistinct. Go through another gate and continue on the track to Wandylaw, which can be seen straight ahead.

A diversion is planned at the farm, which will be well signed. At present this is the route. Where the road bends to the left, go straight ahead through the farm steading, as indicated by the fingerpost – Ellingham 1½ miles – ignore the road to the left. At the end of the buildings turn right by the yellow waymark and walk on for a short distance before turning sharp left, keeping the field boundary on your right. Where the path meets a gravel track cross over and take the footpath straight ahead down the field to the A1 road.

Cross with EXTREME CARE to the footpath opposite and continue over the field to a stile. Cross this and follow the track through gorse bushes and over a plank bridge to a gate. Pass through and follow the track down to Ellingham and the end of the walk – where the Packhorse Inn may be open.

Pack Horse Inn

walk nine
Ellingham to Seahouses

Ellingham
church
lychgate

This walk takes you from Ellingham through the pastoral coastal plain to Beadnell, then up the coast to Seahouses. The route wanders and twists because the rights of way round Beadnell don't run east and west. In spite of this the walk offers gentle going in peaceful country.

It is 11 miles (17.7 km), generally flat but boots are advised for fording the beach stream. There are limited facilities and no public transport at Ellingham, but Seahouses has everything, and funny hats too. If you walk on the beach be aware of the rise or fall of the tide and be careful on slippery rocks.

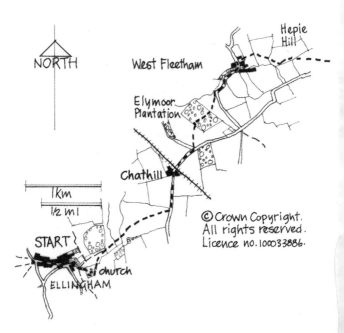

NORTH

West Fleetham

Hepie Hill

Elymoor Plantation

Chathill

1 Km

1/2 ml

START

church

ELLINGHAM

© Crown Copyright. All rights reserved. Licence no. 100033886.

From the Pack Horse
Inn go east along the
road to a T junction.
Go left, keeping straight
on where the main
road bends right. Walk
up to the church, ignoring
a finger post on the left,
go through the lychgate
and round behind the
church to find a narrow
path stepping down
through trees to a footbridge and gate.
   Bear right over a tussocky field to a gate and
stile in the wall. Keep straight on crossing the
footbridge over the Long Nanny, climb the bank
and follow the line of telephone poles through a
long field to a gate in the left-hand corner.
   Go onto the road walking left to Chathill. The
station is on the main East Coast line, with two
trains stopping each way daily. The waiting
room has information on local railway history.
   Follow the B1340 road over the level crossing
and past a large house to a farm track on the
left with a fingerpost – public footpath, West
Fleetham, 1. A wicket gate on the right leads
to a large field. Aim for a gate half way along
Elymoor Plantation, beneath a large oak tree.
   In the wood go sharp left, then sharp right,
following the path which is obstructed towards
the far end. Find your way to the fence,
walking right to a broken wicket gate.

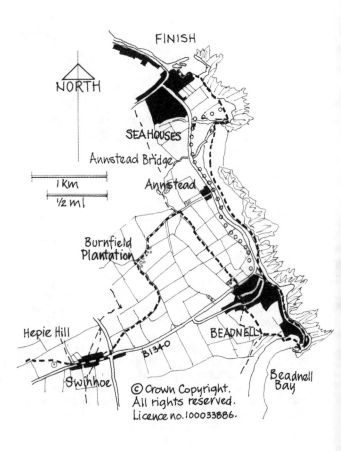

FINISH

NORTH

1 km

½ ml

SEAHOUSES

Annstead Bridge

Annstead

Burnfield
Plantation

Hepie Hill

Swinhoe

B1340

BEADNELL

Beadnell
Bay

Chathill post office

Cross the cultivated field bearing half left to a clump of trees. Behind a large beech is a wicket gate. Ignore the fingerpost and go right to the road, walking left to West Fleetham. At the end of the hamlet you approach terraced cottages, end on to the road. A fingerpost on the right - public footpath, Swinhoe, 1 - directs you along in front of the houses to a stile.

Keep on through two gates then bear half right to a stile in the fence opposite. Go right following the field edge on your right. Just past a field entrance a stile brings you to a large field with traces of rig and furrow ploughing.

Aim to the left of trees round a pond and keep on towards Swinhoe and a gate in the right corner leading onto the road. Walk up past Swinhoe. The road is busy but rights of way through the farm are blocked, so this is the only option.

—approaching Swinhoe

At the cross roads go left for a short distance
to a farm gate on the right with a fingerpost-
public footpath, Annstead, 1¾. Cross the field
diagonally to a gate in the left hand corner,
go through, following the hedge on your left
to a wide gate where the hedge is on your right.
Follow the hedge, curving round to the left to
a stile in a wall. Continue towards Burnfield
Plantation on the right finding a wicket gate
below chestnut trees. Follow the grassy path as
it gradually bears left to reach a gate giving
onto a farm road.

Ignore the right-hand road and keep on
towards Annstead Farm looking out for
waymarked double gates on the right.

At this point the walk can be shortened by
continuing through Annstead to the coast
and walking left to Seahouses.

Otherwise go right at the gates following
the field wall on your right to a gate where
the path crosses to the other side of the wall.
Walk on to a stile, then cross another three fields
and stiles, all in the same direction. A final
stile brings you to a narrow tree strip and a

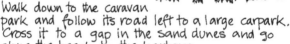
Gable in Beadnell

wooden stile delivers you on to the busy coast road. Cross carefully, going right for 200 yards, then left into Beadnell. Walk through to a T junction and a gated footpath beyond, fingerpost – Lime Kilns and Harbour. Walk down to the caravan park and follow its road left to a large carpark. Cross it to a gap in the sand dunes and go along the beach to the harbour.

Beadnell Bay stretches away south with the Borough boundary running out half way down, with the Long Nanny. You are now in the Northumberland Coast Area of Outstanding Natural Beauty which stretches almost to Berwick.

Beadnell Harbour

From the harbour go left from the kilns, past the turreted house, then left again following the road through the village to its junction with the coast road. (ice cream) There is a choice of routes here. The newly opened Coast Path crosses the road and makes its way through the camp site and continues through fields. At the third field it crosses diagonally to a stile and fingerpost - N - on the coast road. The route then follows the road verge past Seahouses golf clubhouse turning right at the N sign, where it crosses the golf course turning left at the coast to arrive in Seahouses.

Alternatively you can find your way from the road junction through the dunes to the beach if tide conditions are suitable and walk round Annstead Bay to Seahouses.

At the north end of the beach Annstead Burn runs out to the sea. Usually it is a mere trickle but if not go up to the road and over Annstead Bridge.

Fording the burn continue to the sea end of low cliffs where a narrow path leads up to the golf course. Be careful crossing the rocks because they can be slippery.

Cross the golf course on the waymarked path. Look out for flying golf balls. The Coast Route joins from the left and both routes continue to arrive above Seahouses harbour.

Seahouses harbour

walk ten
Seahouses to Belford

Monks House

Walk ten takes you along stretches of 'Northumbria's Lordly Strand', past the capital of Anglo Saxon Northumbria and inland to Belford. It is a walk of 9 miles (15 km) and should take 4 to 5 hours on easy terrain. There is public transport at both ends and facilities at Seahouses, Bamburgh and Belford.

From the centre of Seahouses walk north, taking the road to Bamburgh. At the northern end of the village, where the houses end, find a path to the right, through the dunes on to St. Aidan's Bay and proceed up the beach.

Shortly to your left you will see a group of houses hugging the shore – Monk's House. A stream comes out onto the sand, but it is shallow and easily forded. Later Bamburgh Castle comes into view. It was the capital of the Kingdom of Anglo Saxon Northumbria and the centre of the great cutural flowering known as the Golden Age of Northumbria.

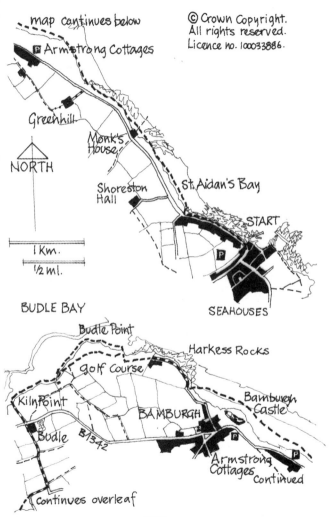

map continues below

Armstrong Cottages

Greenhill

NORTH

Monk's House

Shoreston Hall

St Aidan's Bay

START

1 Km.

1/2 ml.

SEAHOUSES

BUDLE BAY

Budle Point

Harkess Rocks

Golf Course

Kiln Point

BAMBURGH

Bamburgh Castle

Budle

B1342

Armstrong Cottages

continued

Continues overleaf

105

Walk on beyond the castle towards the Harkess Rocks. Veer left and climb to the road, turning right, heading for the lighthouse and walking to the Golf Club House on your left. Fingerpost-  N Coast Path, public bridleway, Budle Point, 3/4.

Here you have a choice. If the tide is well out go down onto the beach and follow it round into Budle Bay with Budle Point on your left. This is the southern limit of the Lindisfarne Nature Reserve. However, if the tide is high follow the right of way, marked with short blue posts, across the golf course, avoiding flying golf balls. Descend through the dunes, heading north-west down towards the shore ignoring a waymark pointing to the left. Follow the shore line round to Kiln Point where you will see a Nature Reserve notice. Budle Bay is a vast stretch of mud flats and salt marsh at low tide. It is a bird watcher's paradise.

At this point turn left on to a grassy track, past cottages on your right, up to the B1342 road.

Bamburgh Castle

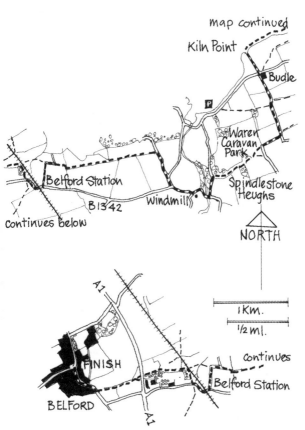

map continued

Kiln Point

Budle

Waren Caravan Park

Belford Station

B1342

Windmill

Spindlestone Heughs

continues below

NORTH

1 Km.

½ ml.

A1

FINISH

continues

Belford Station

BELFORD

A1

Spindlestone Mill

Cross over the road, taking the minor road opposite, passing some recently refurbished farm buildings, now luxury homes. Ignore fingerposts to left and right and after about ⅓ mile turn right into a road leading to Waren Caravan Park. As you approach the entrance a fingerpost- public footpath, Spindlestone Mill, ¾ - directs you through the site to a new wicket gate in the bottom corner and into a field. Go right, through a small wood and two fields and enter woodland on your right. Descend through the trees with Spindlestone Heughs up to the right. This was the setting for the ballad of the Laidley Worm.

"Word went east and word went west
    Word is gone over the sea
That a Laidley worm in Spindleston Heugh
    Would ruin the North Countree."

The giant worm was really a princess from Bamburgh Castle, transformed by her wicked stepmother, but restored by her brother with three kisses.

Coming down onto the road go left to a T junction at a dilapidated mill.

Turn right at the junction and cross the bridge, then climb the hill towards a windmill on the left. Ignore a road coming in from the left and carry on to the B1342. You will see a finger-post for the Coastal Path - N - directing you right and after 100 yards another finger directing you up a minor road where the main road curves right.

A short distance along the minor road a fingerpost on the left - N, public footpath, Station Cottages, 1½, Belford, 2½ - directs you along three fields with rising land on your right. At the end of the third field follow the signs right, then almost immediately left across a field to a gate leading onto a stone track. You are approaching the main east coast railway line. It is safest to turn left, following the track down to the B1342, emerging at whitewashed cottages.

the windmill

the track past the grain silos

Turn right, pass a row of stone cottages and cross the gated level crossing. You will walk on the pavement past the former station. Ahead is a row of brick cottages with a fingerpost just beyond - Public Footpath - Belford 1 - go straight up the stone track, past grain silos on your left, then go left to find a stile and a path leading along the back of more silos on the left.

The path soon reaches the A1 road. CROSS WITH CARE, via the stiles and follow the directions towards Belford with the golf course on your right and its driving range on your left. The path emerges onto the golf club car park. The village lies ahead. Taking a right turn at the golf club gates go along High Street to the village cross and the Blue Bell Inn.

Belford to Holy Island Causeway
Walk Eleven

Walk eleven is an easy 7 miles (11 km) on road, paths and tracks. Short lengths of path can become overgrown in summer and the busy A1 road must be crossed carefully.

Belford has a regular bus service to and from Berwick and Newcastle. A notice on the former bank in the village centre indicates that there are a church, pubs, post office, shops and public toilets.

Start from the market cross, opposite the Blue Bell, an old coaching inn, and walk uphill with the church on your left and the post office on your right. The road was formerly the A 1, but the bypass has transformed it into a quiet country lane. In the reign of Charles I, Belford was described as "the most miserable beggardly town of sods that ever was made in an afternoon, of loam and sticks." Things have improved since then.

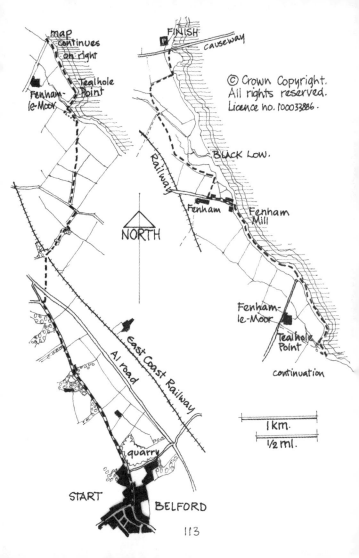

map
continues
on right

FINISH

causeway

Tealhole
Point

Fenham-
le-Moor

© Crown Copyright.
All rights reserved.
Licence no. 100033886.

BLACK LOW.

Railway

Fenham
Mill

Fenham

NORTH

Fenham-
le-Moor

Tealhole
Point

continuation

East Coast Railway

A1 road

quarry

1 km.

½ ml.

START

BELFORD

113

There is a pavement all along the road, but it changes sides occasionally. Cragmill Quarry, on your right, produces crushed whinstone aggregate. Further on, the neo-gothic gateway to Middleton Hall, lies on your left. There are good views of Lindisfarne, the busy A.1 and the East Coast Railway. The wood on the left is thickly carpeted with bluebells in May.

After 1·8 miles (3km) take a track opposite the road to Detchant. Fingerpost– Public Byway. The track soon arrives downhill at the A1 CROSS CAREFULLY (a couple of minutes spent waiting for a gap in the traffic is time well spent). The path continues to a stone bridge over the railway, then through Railway Plantation with Kettle Burn alongside on the left.

the bridge over Foulwork Burn.

About ¼ ml. after the railway bridge look out for a wooden footbridge on the left. Cross the stream, go left for a few yards, then right through a metal farm gate into a broad grassy path between thorn hedges, continuing in a north easterly direction.

At the path end go through a metal gate on to the road. Go left and very soon turn right at metal gates. Fingerpost- Public Bridleway - Fenham-le-Moor. 1¼ ml. Follow the bridleway north-north-east coming into a grass field. Holy Island can be seen straight ahead across Fenham Flats. Pass through a wicket gate and continue on the same line through the next field to reach the shore.

There are alternative routes for a short distance. Firstly go down to the foreshore, following round the high tide line to a high footbridge over Foulwork Burn.

Secondly, if the tide is very high, continue along the edge of the field, then turn right on to the footbridge.

The tidal mud flats are host to many birds, such as visiting Brent and Greylag geese which feed on the abundant inter-tidal plants.

Cross the burn keeping straight on along the shore line to Tealhole Point, where the path goes north-west past a black hut, a posh weekend cabin and a two storey hide at the end of the road from Fenham-le-Moor. Continue along the shore with a choice of grass path or gravel beach. Pass close to Fenham Mill, with the path becoming muddy, but reaching a large yellow notice board just beyond a private slipway. English Nature provides information and byelaws for the Lindisfarne Nature Reserve. Go up a short path between trees behind the notice board, arriving on the road. Continue towards Fenham, passing houses on your right and opposite farm buildings turn right on to a path. Fingerpost - Holy Island Causeway - 1½ ml.

the two storey hide

Fenham Mill

Go through a metal farm gate, bearing left, round
a large stone barn and continuing with a fence and
hedge on your left. At the end of the rather swampy
field there is a stile on the left where St. Cuthbert's
Way joins our route. Ignore it and find a stile on
your right. Cross a small bridge over Beal Cast and
another stile. Now, following St. Cuthbert's Way,
cross the next field diagonally to a wide gap in the
hedge with a metal gate. A wide path, fenced
on both sides, soon brings you to a footpath
on the right leading to a new wicket gate and the
foreshore. Turn left, walking between huge
concrete blocks, the remains of W.W.2. defences,
to reach the Holy Island Causeway. The walk
ends at the car park.

A bus service operates between Berwick and
Holy Island, but it is tide-dependent. So times
vary.

If you have time and the tide is right (see
table of safe crossing times) a visit to the
island is recommended.

117

Holy Island Causeway to Berwick
walk twelve

the path from the causeway

The twelfth and final section of the walk round Berwick Borough starts at the Holy Island Causeway and follows the coast up to the starting point at Berwick. There are tracks and minor roads along the coast and when the tide is low golden sands make easy walking, however care should be taken at Cheswick and Cocklawburn where slippery shelving ridges of rock run out to sea. Even more care should be taken at Goswick where notices warn of quicksands and unexploded bombs!

The walk is 10 miles (16km.) and it can be walked in about 5 hours. There are no facilities until you reach Spittal.

From the car park at the causeway walk north between the concrete blocks of W.W.2. defences. You are now following the newly created Coastal Path, part of the developing pan-European North Sea Trail, with its distinctive logo, 'N'.

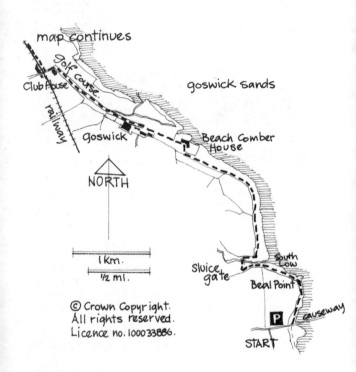

map continues

golf course

Club House

railway

goswick

goswick sands

Beach Comber House

NORTH

1 km.

½ ml.

© Crown Copyright.
All rights reserved.
Licence no. 100033886.

Sluice gate

South Low

Beal Point

P

causeway

START

120

Beyond the blocks continue along the shore, turning left round Beal Point. The public right of way actually runs on top of the low cliffs, but there are unprotected trenches in the long grass and the safest policy is to keep to the shore.

Continue up the South Low, now on grass, towards the sluice gates in the distance, keeping alongside the fence on your left. Go up the grassy bank turning right along a gravel path to the Beal Sluice. Go through two wicket gates and follow more gravel path as it swings right.

The track reverts to grass, following the coast inside the dunes, with broad views and skylarks serenading your progress. There are two gates across the way near Beachcomber House,

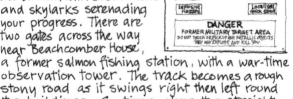

a former salmon fishing station, with a war-time observation tower. The track becomes a rough stony road as it swings right then left round the buildings. Continue along the straight road, passing Coastguard Cottage on your right and Goswick Farm on your left.

Beal Sluice

Goswick Farm

An old local rhyme explains that mainland farms supplied Lindisfarne Priory with food —
"From Goswick we've geese, from Cheswick we've cheese;
From Buckton we've venison in store;
From Swinhoe we've bacon, but the Scots have it taken,
And the prior is longing for more."

As the road becomes public it passes the links of Goswick Golf Club. Pass the clubhouse and go left with the road towards the railway. Turn right just before the level crossing (fingerpost, Coastal Path) following the railway fence on your left. At the end of the field go right for a short distance, turning left though a kissing gate and shortly through another kissing gate to join a grass track straight ahead running parallel to the fence on your left.

At the Cheswick road end go straight on through two metal gates to follow a gravel path. You will reach a gate marked "Private Land", with a stile alongside. On the left is a pond with fishing stages. To the right the fields

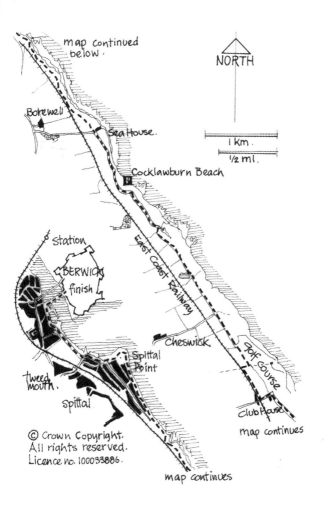

map continued
below.

NORTH

1 km.
½ ml.

Bolewell

Sea House.

Cocklawburn Beach

P

East Coast Railway

Station

BERWICK

finish

Tweed mouth.

Spittal

Spittal Point

Cheswick

Golf Course

Club House

map continues

map continues

are full of wild flowers, particularly cowslip and bloody cranesbill. A prominent mound appears ahead - an old lime kiln with ramped access from the south and a W.W.2 concrete pill box on top. The path arrives at twin gates and bends right to meet the road. Go left following the road to Cocklawburn Beach, a popular summer playground. Beyond the beach are cliffs which stretch all the way to Spittal. In the distance is the distinctive silhouette of Sea House.

Follow the road uphill, over a cattle grid, to Sea House, where it goes left to a railway crossing. Your route continues straight on, Fingerpost - Public Byway, Spittal 1 3/4, Coast Path, . Go between wind-bent trees to another cattle grid with a wicket gate at the side.

The cliff top path leads on to Spittal with the railway never far away on the left and wide views over Berwick Bay. Ahead lies the exclamation mark of the lighthouse at the end of Berwick Pier. At a further cattle grid go through the wicket gate and in about 200 yards find steps going down to the right, to Spittal Promenade.

Cocklawburn Beach

Spittal Promenade

The prom was rebuilt recently as a heightened sea defence. Half way along, the Venetian Pavilion has refreshments and public conveniences round the back.

At the end of the prom your path goes round Spittal Point, where the old industrial buildings have mostly been demolished, leaving the tall brick chimney as a splendid landmark. From the car park on the point follow the road round to the left, crossing another car park diagonally to a stony road which comes out on to the main road.

Go right towards Tweedmouth and Berwick. You will now see Berwick across the River Tweed with its defensive walls and the three bridges.

The road passes the lifeboat station and the Carr Rock Jetty, then leads on to Tweedmouth Dock with a wide grass strip alongside. Pavements take over in Tweedmouth and at the end of Main Street the road bends right leading you on to Berwick Bridge, which was built in 1611-34 at the suggestion of James VI and I, when he came south to assume the English throne.

Across the bridge you arrive at Bridge End, your original starting point. There are seats where you can take a well-earned rest and there is a pub on the corner.

Notes

Also published by Berwick Ramblers
BERWICK WALKS
twenty-four walks within a twelve
mile radius of Berwick, written
and illustrated by Arthur Wood.
ISBN 0-9545331-0-0 (978-0-9545331-0-6)

Notes